Bone

Thomas Simpson

Bone Picker

Acknowledgements

Poems in this collection have previously appeared in *Voiceworks*,
Creatrix, *Axon*, *Westerly* and *Pulped Fiction: an anthology of microlit*.

This book was written on Whadjuk Noongar land.
The author pays respect to the traditional owners and the
continuation of their culture.

Bone Picker
ISBN 978 1 76109 302 9
Copyright © text Thomas Simpson 2022
Cover image: Mostafaft Shots from Pexels

First published 2022 by
GINNINDERRA PRESS
PO Box 3461 Port Adelaide 5015
www.ginninderrapress.com.au

Contents

1

Marcoola

Cooling after the day-long
drive from Guyra,
the bonnet ticks
slowly, like a dying metronome.
Behind the dunes, night creeps
up the collars of the banksias.
With a drop in light,
the onshore winds bite
sweat of our necks
and backs. The sea smells
sweet after two months
working in an earthy waft
of cow shit on wet grass
and damp leather whips.
I am more comfortable
dragging my feet
through the dry white sand
still warm on the surface.

You keep your boots
on, ambivalent, rolling
a cigarette. Tucked into
the steep rise of the dune,
between the saltbush and aloe,
we take long swigs
from a jug
of tawny. Our severance
package. Unfazed
by planes descending
into Maroochydore airport,

a small flock
of black-tailed gulls feed
on pippies, moving down the beach
with the wind. They remind
me of the cattle
we drove, licking up great tufts
of grass with muscular
velcro tongues.

With sand in your beard
and tawny forming
a stain on your lip
you say,
I feel good having nothing
at all to do.

Uncle

You sit, grey
like the meals
the nurse pours
down your peg tube.
Under dim hospice light
you show me your entry wounds
blotted with claret
and yellow-brown stains
of disinfectant,
and your healed scars
that melted the muscles
and tattoos on your
back and shoulders. You smile
and show off
these badges of honour.
A consolation prize,
while the doctors
pack it in before your long nap
in the dirt.

Flyscreen

My brother's feet
leave passing pads
of sweat
on the asbestos veranda.
Late becomes
too late
as we stand
either side of a flyscreen threshold.
He is shuffling
through the heat
of grief. I stay inside, cool
in my denial.

A Wake at the Five-Ways Hotel

Questions of blood
and lineage, a mis-stepped
pronoun during mourning
and grog
leads to violence
in the gravel car park.

Bells and boom gates –
coal trains from the west,
cane crushers from the north –
suck away
the thud
of an unknowing stranger
hitting the deck; whimpers
of a grieving mother
as drunk sons point
the finger; arm-length pleading
with shirt collars
bunched in fists.

Onlookers seasoned
by scuffle are pacified
by the heavy machines
that never fail
to shake the walls
of the Five-Ways Hotel.

Tank

On the embankment
we shed
our school shirts, so the parents
don't know, and puff away
the smokes we foraged all week, shoved
into a crumpled Stuyvesant
soft-pack. Shivering, we climb
down onto the water tank in your neighbour's yard.

Floodlights outside
the Drayton Hotel pull
the sun down to take its place behind
livestock trucks barrelling
down from Wyreema. The whistle
of dry grass and wild oats
being combed
from the highway's shoulder
washes over the lazy paddock.

We scoff
at the workers who stumble
to their utes to rile
the dogs in back, mock the Harleys
in tight leather who take
their place. Up
on that tank we think
we're waiting it out, for the city,
for adulthood – shirtless
and trying to work the cap
off our longneck on the edge
of a brittle concrete
tank.

I spent my twenty-second year at a stolen glass desk

watching
the static outdoor lives
shown in the honeycombed balconies
of the new flats
across the road, I pick
at the dirt under my fingernails
and the burnt
skin on my arms. Fading
beach towels and nylon
washing lines shake
in the afternoon northerly
as buses scrape
green didactic signs on Lutwyche Road.
Forgotten beer cans and sacrificial
coffee mugs become overloaded ashtrays
under stained and curling
books from the local branch library:
>   fought migraines
>   reading Nietzsche; chuckled
>   looking over my shoulder
>   reading Bukowski.
Half-baked poems, scenes
of living scrawled on red and white
parcel pick-up cards:
>   *please collect your parcel*
>   *from Toowong DC, Indooroopilly*
>   *Post Shop, St Lucia LPO.*

Watch, drink, burn
ash until the mosquitos
start to bite my toes
and yell in my ears.
A photo of my grandparents
and that flash new degree look
down at me both growing
dust and frayed corners
on the windowsill. Discontent
mixes with spilt Fourex
and cheap weed, while I watch
possums slowly climb the powerlines
hand over hand from the new flats
to our lopsided
Queenslander. Their gruesome
shadow cast big as a man
on the quiet sheen
of new bitumen.

Look at the People Leaving

Light from the street lamps
outside the window, blurred
by the half-drawn blinds,
paints her skin
with yellowy stripes
that illuminate
the tiny white hairs
of her bare arms
and shoulders.
I lean, groggy
in the door frame,
my ear pressed
hard against the jamb
listening to the pipes
and gutters gush
with summer rain.
I look past her, down
from our perch on Shorncliffe
out to Moreton Bay
where the clouds frown
against the sea,
at the yachts and dinghies
that cut and tear
through the brown, muddy swell,
at the people leaving.

Ceduna

Whipped up
off rippling corrugations, bight sand nips
and gathers at my ankles. I hold the barbed
wire apart and crouch
through the fence as it hums
and cracks in the wind. Her thongs
shovel soft sand onto her calves
and into the rolled cuffs
of her jeans, while she finds rocks
to chock our trailer.

The spinifex stings
less now. Our days
without shoes
and phone reception tally.

Transcontinental

Finger dips in her opaque glass of Mundrabilla roadhouse plonk.
Calmly lifts drunk fruit fly to safety. Lets him dry
on a serviette, wonders how long till he'll fly off.

Littered nuts off arthritic salmon gums crack and skip under tyre. I sit,
feet on dash, lifting long strips of skin frail as wet paper.
Raw pink under burnt salty knees.

Sleet gathered in gutters and sills of our hinterland home
dripped onto the veranda. Across the desert sand is our ruin
and the shallow buried memories in a grassless backyard.

Thirsty

Flying out of Perth
in a giant steel duck,
wings flapping
in ascent. Shaking
off evening dew.

The eastern suburbs
look thirsty
and hard.
Fenced by powerlines, cul-de-sac
fossils etch
through dust reserves.

The man
next to me sucks
sticky date pudding
from his fingernails.

Native North

My father tires
of Melbourne. Tight lanes
and peach-tin trams.
He wears his suitcase
down a wind-tunnelled Fitzroy lane,
sounding like a plastic sail,
his spray jacket
sleeves whipping and cracking
behind.

He's not worn
shoes this long
on a weekend since his wedding.
How has my brother
taken to this cold
crowded city? Why have I run
to the sandy west?
Why do we deny
our native north?

Glass House Mountains

He belongs
to this island.
His scratched
and spotted shins
hold up the sagging pier,
mix with mangrove
antennae and melaleuca leaves.
His pumice-stone chest
invites the setting sun
and unbeatable sandfly.
His clouded eyes
house those three
glass mountains drawing
their silhouette against sugar cane smoke.

The mountains' shadow
bleeds over the wound
of waterfront mansions
to the north,
their foundations cracking
and sinking
into the ancient wetland and scars
of the old sand mine.

Tibrogargon shows
her sloping face
to the muddy passage
and bore-pocked island.

Pulling on his amber
longneck, Bob tongues
a fisherman's friend
where his front teeth
used to be.

In the Shell Motel

Indian ocean glare
claws tears from
corners of squinted eyes.
A crack in the windscreen
widens on misjudged ruts
and curtains of sand.
Scratched by a key
into splintered lead paint
of a doorless iron husk
– the shell motel.
Corrugated walls growl
in the wind,
reverberating through
tin cups and chipped jars
left and lined
by each tenant
– sardines from Porto
– peanuts from Queensland
– Italian tomatoes
Smell the world
in the shell motel.
Djiti djiti sweeps
corners and walls
sifting a feed
from ash and forgotten tea leaves.

Red sand
on skin.
Red sand
in swag.
The ocean laughs
white foam spewing
out of its jagged smile
as I dream of rain
in the shell motel.

Shark Bay

Crackling amplifier
and dull awes
of a dolphin feeding
down the beach
at Monkey Mia.
A mid-west morning storm
bleeds rain through my swag
pressing heavy
on my face and toes.
Despondent repetition
of the road home
seems crueller.

Impressions

Don't follow the ground birds,
the old fella says. *Mischief*
birds, they'll lead you astray.

Swallows and wagtails dart
past my head, clicking their wings;
blue against the rain-pocked sand.

Hardened by shell and rock
my feet slip into damp, soft
tyre tracks. Even out here, under

my own steam, trying
for some sort of natural reset,
there's comfort in the straightness
of their line, of machines' impression
between scrub and sea.

Blue Gum Breeze

Sweet, resiny breeze
from shifting piles of glue gum pulp
flogs the white caps cresting
through Shoal Bay, stipples
the upturned keels lined on the shore
with spray.

Gently prodding fatigued herring
in a bucket splattered
with dry cement, a young boy fans
their dorsal fins as they bob
morbidly in the rusted, bloody water.

The man next to him pins
a blowfish under his rubber thong
to retrieve the hook. Its gills grind
with oxygen as it puffs out
its barbs in defence
against the splintered jetty.
A muted giggle breaks the silent pair
as the bloated by-catch is booted
back to the drink.

2

Bone Picker

The port's red and white
cranes lose
detail in the rising heat
off steel containers
and bitumen,
become thick
textured strokes
of pastel colour
like Nolan's desert trees.

Retractable claws pick
the bones
of leviathan ships
and pile
them by their latticed
shins. Instruments of money
shimmer softly in sheep shit
and diesel fumes
that bubble
on the Indian Ocean.

Cockburn Sound

Madness of the full
moon drives
anglers onto footholds
in the rocks. Whispers
of cocky salmon
and snapper
have men hiding
their rigs and bait. Desperate
casts and whipping rods
reflect the yellow lamplight
of empty vessels
waiting their turn
at Coogee.

The dead water speaks
of change – fingers
of the old-timer
pleading down the line,
reading
the sea floor – newcomer's
hands on hips
feeling hard-done-by
while his patient partner
gently wipes
the light rain
from her phone.

I've come to hate this wind

You're not supposed to hate
an icon. But it blows me into bouts
of homesickness, carrying storms
over town away to the hills and robs
me of sleep with the spindly lick
of dry bottlebrush against my window.
Yet it beats the humid bowl
I crawled out from.

Carrington Street

Shrieks and yells aren't uncommon
down our street. A skirmish
of broken glass and torn-off
hubcaps paint the footpath
and sandy verge from the TAB,
past our place, down
to the service station.

She unloads
great echoing howls
in the shadow
behind a petrol bowser.
We follow the screams
our feet rushing
with the crescendo
of suffering. Neighbours
whisper and point
behind wire fences,
locked screen doors.

She is under
your arm, sucking in
shaky short
breaths. You ask
her name and gently dabs
at the ballooning
split and run off
from her shattered nose.
I am frozen
by her instinctual
readiness to help,
standing with a wooden spoon
still dripping
with pasta water,
my bare socks
mopping the multicoloured
diesel pools.

Meditations at a Kitchen Table

You sip
sweet pinot
pinky neatly tucked
around the stem.
Hemp lip balm
leaves a perfect print
on the glass.
You say the cheese
has mould. I've missed
bin day, again.

Aluminium blinds
etch their grooves
into the plastered
window frame. The beer
in the fridge
halfway gone
before cooled.
Grubby hands smudge
the amber bottle.

Hangovers are worse
now we can afford
to stay out.
An untouched meal. Fruit bowl
full of panadol.
We smoke
to avoid saying
something honest.

The fridge leaks
a strange smell, but holds
only condiments.
Calendar magnet
counts your absence.

The storm doesn't start.
hard-baked desert
air pushes cloud out
to sea past the port's swinging
cranes. I miss
the storms
we had up north
when the tin roof would sing
with pelting rain.
Cracks of thunder made
light fixtures
shake. Soaking possums
came to our table
on the veranda
and we'd feed
them with flat palms.

Rubbish in Waiting

Rosemary sprigs lose
their perch next
to names of fallen,
still remembered. Afternoon
wind rips
up Monument Hill,
torments the cellophane
wrappers around
flowers – now sodden
and bleeding colour –
piled at the base
of the war memorial.

Brady left his medals
in the back of the drawer
and slept in
past dawn.
It's all rubbish
in waiting, he says
as we round the visitor's
lens now turned
to the sea; the sun slips
away behind North Mole.

Blackboy Hill

Twenty-eights and galahs drop
husks on the bore-water-stained
memorial. Four steel arches stand
over the digger's rising sun, adopting
the rosy tint of late spring suburbia. Only two
balga grass trees stand now, arthritic
in this arranged landscape.

A jogger does a double take
spotting me on the bench
covered in parrot shit
and white ants, surprise at another actor
in the silent world
outside her headphones.
The painted-over plaque reads,
rest and reflect. She pauses to time
her heart and runs on
past the sparse reeds
of the old balgas
and through the empty car park
reserved for hundreds.

Pageantry

Utes adorned with accessories
from catalogue covers and backyard
engineers – whimsical sideshow
beasts of checker plate and rattle can – whip
the dam's edge. Foamed water supply
and discarded marron shells spew
out of their wheel arches. The pissing contest
perpetuates with new arrivals, unhitching
jet skis and speedboats
from trailers while their children, still struggling
with seatbelts and sidebars, scramble out
onto the warm, muddy sand. Men bristle
at the tremor and wake
of machines, eager to join the pageantry –
sunburnt, tattooed plumage
on oily, fibreglass peacocks.

Sitting on our swags
up the hill, behind the creek's skeletal memory.
We watch lifejackets and watercraft change
hands while the sun silhouettes
a stand of drowning melaleuca
and ruffled parrots turn
over leaves and bottle caps, pleading
for crumbs, for a feed.

Here in the suburbs, semis roar
and squeal as they line
up for the port. My feet
caked with mud and swollen from march flies
grubbying the wall, I think
about the twenty-eights' greasy, dull
collar as my daily visitor
the red wattlebird sifts
through gutters on the back shed.

The Swap

Family SUVs squeak over speed bumps and thread back onto the highway. They had time on the way south to sample chocolate and wine from deceased industry towns now opt for fast food and faster speed limits of the highway home. Some grimace empathetically at my open bonnet, grease covered hands. In this beehive of movement, I see others left static. Two boys quietly resigned to their burgers and chips. Unkempt hair and muddied feet show the wilful fatigue of a weekend out of town. Their father doesn't eat, fiddles with his phone. It beeps and he's up, pats their heads and leaves. The older boy watches him adjust his shorts by the dusty ute. A woman takes up a seat. The younger takes in her greeting, doesn't notice their backpacks at her feet. She pinches a chip from the older who still watches the ute. He takes in the scene bordered in grey plastic of the rear-view mirror, bows his head, slides the ute into gear. The RAC van pulls up. Roadside assistance now inconvenient, I look beyond the mechanic's baldness for a second thought, an embrace, a tear. I see the playground now faded and derelict, the dull brick service centre resurfaced with smooth marble and glass.

High Street Squat

Orange claws scrape
splintered jarrah beams
into piles under the few white gums
they have spared. Oil container
terrariums hanging from streetlights
and chalk mandalas on the pavement
now lonely oddities
of former freedom.

Overloaded vans and wagons line
the gravel verge at Booyeembara reserve.
Refugees of irony –
saving the wetlands at Beeliar flattened
their squat to a roundabout.

Peering through flood lights
at the damp turned earth
and half-buried prayer flags, I startle
the fluorescent security guard
dozing on his lunchbox.

Portrait of a neighbour

It's warmer outside
than in. Lines of sunlight bleed
through gnarled acacia
like glowing bars on a space heater
onto the dewy sand and grass.

The old woman across
the street is being dragged
by a yellowing lap dog
toward her yellowing asbestos fence.

A door on the Anglicare hatchback
swings open as she struggles,
fingers purpling, with the padlocked gate.
The contractual visitor pulls
on a fleece and sighs, kneeing
the car door shut.

Firewood's been stacked
high against the shed since lockdown started – leaning
into the cold snap, might be her last.

3

Rare Showing of Sun

Away from tight cobble
and tarmac footpaths, sitting
on a rock wall that falls unending
into a frigid North Sea, I screech at seagulls
the size of small dogs
my eyes heavy in a binge
of relaxed open container laws. Touristic
ambition evaporating
along with the fog rolling off from Gipsy Brae
under a rare showing of sun.

Boys in matching tracksuits
crouch down in the long grass of a forgotten playground
arguing the best design
for an Irn-Bru can bong.

Caledonian Best

Close coldness in a city of greys. Grey granite blocks lift out
the harbour in Aberdeen and produce grey people with hard
quarried eyes. Old blokes tell old stories to me of
minute-long geography with many older names. They speak
fast but say little. Ash carpet tongues lick tobacco stained
moustaches at the sight of my airport-fresh twenty quid.
Patience stretches for my languid drawl just long enough for
a shout. I resort to talking to my foamy pint of Caledonian
Best about screeching birds and the warmth of home.
Grateful for its quiet attention, and the old chair with the
arse fallen out.

Interstitial

Left over space
undevelopable
between brasserie, cop shop
and motorway.

Kids comb
piles of trash
for objects of interest.

Police lean on vans
sharing cigarettes
with left over people.

An old woman
knots her heavy brow
straightening
a print of Jesus hanging
from a tag
on her faded canvas tent.

Stereotypes

The drunk Frenchman prods
me for exoticisms
of coastline and bush. Smoke drifts
out of his toothy smile as he muses
on each syllable – koo-k-a-bur-ra
and laughs, slapping my arm.

I point to the crop
and scrub across the railway line, ask
what grows here – what are the trees named?
I don't know, corn? Who cares?
he says, I just live here.
Have you seen the pl-at-y-pus?

Like his colonial countrymen
Peron and Lasueur who painted
and named and fucked off, we are left
with stereotypes – a long-skirted woman pedals
past the bar
with fresh baguettes cradled
gently under her arm.

Bells

Thin lanes snake from the sea – gathering
up brick and blue tile
polished by the sensible
sandals of paying
and pious tourists – up to the bleeding saints and fat cherubs
of an Alfama church. Its bells mimicked
by howling dogs in beer-soaked
shopfronts and the uneasy
swaying of old veiled women on window railings
fumbling rosary beads
with tears in their eyes and sardine blood under their fingernails.

Watching Strangers, Jardim do Marques

A young boy gathers bottle tops
from the feet of men
playing cards
on makeshift tables in the plaza – they live on
as marbles, spinning tops and surgical tools
for moths meandering too long
in the hanging mist
of the water fountain.

Sarumawashi

Patrons laugh
and drink beer
while tired, grey macaques don
papier mâché masks
and dance
like pantomime dolls with jolting
hands and feet. Some lean
in for pictures
with smiles that quickly turn
at a tightened grip
or wandering hand, pacified
by the trainer's boot
on the milk-crate stage.

Some of the first

Couldn't afford the flight to make the funeral. Instead my mother sets the scene by phone, her boots crunching dead grass on the way back to her car, cockatoos and ravens arguing in dying old gums as she counts gravestones baring her maiden name. Births and deaths before federation. Some of the first white fellas to split the land in the Lockyer Valley – *Fruit bowl of South-east Queensland.* This is my mother's home, not mine. I remember being sent out there as a child one dry winter and came back early with dust in my lungs and my eyelashes rubbed clean off. She filed for divorce and shipped us up to the tropics – we've all run from this place and our blood memory of tilling red soil and holding our breath for rain. The earthy smell of brushed potatoes and cut cabbage stuck in my clothes.

Jet lag

Shivering in the afternoon wind
minutes out of bed. My brain
has a second-long delay
like a poorly dubbed film.
The beer is too cold.
I feel it wind its way down.
Your eyes weigh with age, not sleep,
they plead for stories of youth and trouble. Something
to transport you back
to the Europe you saw at my age.
As recent memory tickles
of the substance-heavy trip,
the white and red bodies of the grandstand
and the oval shake
the gnarled old fig trees above
so, we turn to the game.
All I can offer
is a Portuguese cigarette.

4

Outside Cloisters Square

Sensor light beads
through hundreds of holes
in the aluminium roller door
that leads to Cloisters Square.
Crawling in mechanical waves
up the battered steel mesh
of my blue trolley
like ants before rain.
Still hours from dawn
the upward moving bars
of light make the trolley leap
forward and dizzy me
rocking back on the heels
of my boots.

The man with the matted beard
screams at his reflection
in the door of a French patisserie
every morning I'm there.
Except the days
the bins are bathed
on the sidewalk,
the wheels of my blue trolley
slipping and tracking
through yesterday's almond milk lattes
and gluten-free granola.
I stop avoiding
eye contact with him.
Between his rants
he looks sure of himself.

By my third lap
white collars leak
off buses and fill
the cafés and juice bars
laughing to one another
or thumbing phones.
The man with the matted beard
trades his screams
for whispers to the cuff
of his khaki jacket.
He gazes upward
at Brookfield Towers airbrushed
with morning amber.

Last Tuesday, I saw him
darting between two steel bins
catching fresh cigarette butts
to salvage millimetres
of tobacco he'd tightly roll.
I offered him a fresh pinch
from my pouch.
Now he runs
up and down Hay Street
to the steel bins
and the red Post van
outside Cloisters Square.

Pulling Teeth

At eye level
scuffed shoes and fallen
socks pass under the frosted glass
in misdirected excitement
on their way
to the station.
The dentist lists
caried and missing teeth. Her high
cheekbones and fluorescent teeth
close to glassed eyes
as she prods
a brown molar.

The local anaesthesia
is stealing my tongue,
air conditioning cracking
my throat. I forget
to ask for a medical certificate
before the pressure
of vice-grips
rings in my ears,
already missing
the day's pay.
Virginia Trioli speaks
too fast
for the closed captions
behind the dentist's
straining arms.
We've changed prime minister.

The woman sucking
spit shows me
in a small plastic mirror
how to brush my teeth,
How many cigarettes
do you smoke per day?
while the charms
of her white-gold
bracelet brush my chin
and the abandoned grips.
Did you know
that working-class
Australians have seven
fewer teeth
than professionals?
I shrink
in the horizontal
chair, wishing to hide
behind the paper bib.

After stitching the gum
the dentist folds
a brochure on private health
and a tube of toothpaste
with the invoice.
She points to the reception
like a roadworker
waving through traffic
while I smear
torrents of blood over
my numbed face
with a sodden tissue.

At Karrakatta station
transit officers stop
the train to kick off
a man with a shopping trolley.
He fans the officer's face
with his valid ticket. Holding
the door with my boot
I spit
the ballooning gauze
and gob-full of blood
into a rusting
steel bin. The transit officer
drops a carbon copy
of the shopper's fine.

37°C Outside State Library of WA

Pink flushed faces
and squeaking
hot rubber thongs
make their way over
the footbridge and file
through the gaps
between the hulking grey
institutions. The steel handle
of my mail cart
starts to burn
and crust with dry sweat.
Last night's wine
steals my saliva
and leaks out of my pores,
collecting in the folds
of my faded work shirt.

A boy leans
his ice cream cone
in offering. The drippings
soak the serviette
wrapper, run through
his chubby white fingers
and paint his velcro sandals.
Someone has trowelled
sunscreen across his face.
He smells like primary school –
sharp pencils, stale piss
and pungent whiff
from the adhesive back
of a sticker. A woman hisses
the boy back
to arm's length.
Her eyes dart
to misinterpret the scene.

We Sit

Cyclists parade past
their clip-in shoes
clacking on the pavement
like lycra-clad
clydesdales.
We sit
edged on the doorstep
of Leederville post office
as sunlight starts to filter
through gaps in tall
government offices,
light up still lives
of ornamental homewares
and sheen
off freshly painted
public art.
We sit
Harpreet's broad brown
feet stretch out in front,
his gnarled and yellowing
toenails curling
to the early morning warmth.
His feet expose a life
lived outside – deep cracks
and calloused knuckles.
My feet have grown pink
and soft, nails clipped
down to the skin,
ground smooth
under rigid, steel-toed boots.

We sit
and sip the bitter tea
he brings home
from Punjab. My misdirected
smoke sifts
through the wisps
of his white beard
under his ambivalent smile.
We sit
but stand out –
his lazily tied turban
and shirt inside out,
my grimy hi-vis
and scuffed boots –
in this leafy suburb
of cold drip coffee
and ochre cobbled paths.
We sit
on that little
doorstep, our legs
in the sun.

Weld Square

Some sit cross-legged
talking quietly. Others curl
up, dozing in clumps
of mottled shape
under Norfolk Island pines.

City of Perth aim
their sprinklers, collect
wrappers and deflated silver sacks.

Council workers,
yellow shirts stretched thin
over heaving torsos, faces
pink and creased
with discontent. Move
the sleepers on.

The sleepers hoist on crutches
and struggle
on collapsed bare feet,
regroup on the footpath
and move down Stirling Street
then over the train line
to Royal Perth, check
the waitlist to see
who else made the trip.

Two at a Time

The boss has her eye
on him now. His empty bay
among the busy morning clatter
and chat. He's taken to smoking
two at a time, while three middle-aged
higher ups escort
the reception clerk over to Northbridge,
chip in for the coffee she likes, baying
like lap dogs that'll turn
on each other in a second, all thinking
they have a shot.

Vacuum

Another storm
that doesn't hit,
sweeps over the eastern
hills. Faint shards
of lighting pass
the windows above
our mail sorting frames.
You share my longing
for the north,
for weather. Your brown calloused hands –
still holding on
to the next letter –
shape the gorges
of home, paint Kununurra's
broad flats steaming
after evening torrents.

Feet

at Moore River Native Settlement

Scorched earth
cleared and fenced
in perpetual vacancy.
Ash-covered
stones stipple
contours in the plain
like children's feet
turning over the soil
as they run
down
to Mogumber Mission.

A lone stand
of banksia,
its wintered bulbs
staring at me, like dark
unblinking eyes
of those buried
by conflicted history
and the banality
of procedural evil.

Frangipani

Buses hiss
through flooded drains
down Beach Street,
throwing arcs
of gritty water
into my shoes.
A container ship teases
my hangover
with its foghorn
and I miss the curb.
I lay soaked
like forgotten laundry.
I can taste
the oil-slick rainbows
around a frangipani
all waterlogged
and rotting
next to my head.
My mother wore
them in her hair
sometimes. She'd even let
honeybees swim
through the golden strands
as they inspect
one freshly plucked
from the tree out front.

Three years on

and a different desk
with a hand-turned wooden ashtray.
I like to let the ember settle
after the tobacco is burnt
for the sugary smell
of burnished linseed oil. The same
old photograph of my grandparents continues
to look over my toil, folded rejections
and feedback stuffed in a cut-open
old goon box. Another degree on a different coastline
and I spend my time
still staring out the window
watching as the cool change
comes in from the sea.
Sheets of rain move
through the ghost gums, rattling
the neighbour's grapevine
and muddies the dusty, hot
window. Stray drops permeate
the flyscreen and pepper the job seeker form,
photocopied ink bleeding
onto the sill.

On Tick

I still wear my work shirt
when I drive to Port Beach
and sit out the day. Containers pile
up while waves peel
off the groin. I bought wine
on credit, half an ounce
on tick. Won't last long
before I ask for my job back.
The hours were long
and the pay was shit, but it beats
reusing roaches and telling people
you write
poetry.

News

News of my father's second divorce
makes me think of his first.
Over soupy home brew he speaks
of financial stress and how to use an electronic
signature, while I try to remember
my childhood home. The red tin roof
loud as a pipe band
in ubiquitous summer storms.
The bay window looking
over the Maroochy and highway
and steel bench where that girl
with a constant black eye would sit.

You know, I could have sold
it for more, if I had more time.
Fill us up?

Lines on the back of mum's thighs
from the plastic lawn chair
when she'd stretch the landline out the kitchen window –
the drawer she hid Pall Mall slims.

Me old mate Marshall and the Fijian bloke
next door had to help
me clean up under the house.

Where I would hide and poke
around with the fossilised lizards
and green rat pellets
when the voices got loud, feet heavy,
the solid thud and clink of longnecks
piling up – like they are tonight.

It seemed too tall and lopsided, fragile
chamfer boards held together by layers of paint
and not much else, the day we left with that bloke
with shiny, crowned teeth.
A cardboard suitcase
on my lap.

First Frogs of Evening

I push
off hands and knees
as treated pine stumps
shrink
with the incline
of the block, empty
my lungs
to squeeze
below splintered beams.
Impressions
of my baby-fat
hands, clear
from times before
in the powdery lime
Mum says
not to touch.
The house rests
on my back
rising and falling
with each breath,
my chest spreads
out on tacky clay.
The first frogs
of evening
quiet
tearing voices,
heavy feet.

toeprints on the wall

rain stipples the dusty, salt-sprayed window
percussive echo of sandy feet on floorboards
memory clad in bore-stained fibro

a wattlebird picks a feed out of cobwebbed flyscreen
taps rusted shut; all the copper's been nicked

curtains dance like flowing skirts in the afternoon wind
shifting sand that settles and builds in forgotten corners

nicotine-stained paint above his father's favourite chair
children's dirty toeprints up their old bedroom wall

whiff of stale beer, smashed stubbies on the floor
mix with the bent spoons and blankets of a squatter's old nook

skin burnt and taut under his half-drunk tears
after walking the shore of a forgotten boom town

Hourly Updates

At KSP Writers' Centre

The hive of djilyaro
outside the window imitates
the uneven drum and hiss
of hydraulic brakes and heavy tyres
on Great Eastern Highway
over the hill. They mock
me in their hard work while I sit, listening
to the hourly updates
of the Claremont serial killer trial
and finger condensation gathering
on my beer. The ghost of Katherine's
heavy catalogue exists in this massive
jarrah desk and the tinder-dry mulch
audibly crackling in the first sting
of summer, alongside the intricate lattice
cladding her namesake
colonial homestead.

About the Author

Thomas Simpson is a poet and sound artist based in Western Australia. He was a participant in the 2019–20 *Westerly* Writers' Development Program and is a committee member of WA Poets Inc. Thomas is currently completing a PhD at Deakin University, combining poetry and soundscape ecology in south-west WA. His poetry has appeared in various publications throughout Australia, in print and online. This is his first poetry collection.